Mindset Masters
Volume One

Walt Disney

David John W.StClair

DEDICATION

This book and all other products belonging to this series are dedicated to everyone who wants to make a difference in this world, determined to make this world a better place and their own life a piece of art.

There once was a vision and a dream. I did believe in it with all my heart. My determination, clear intent and perseverance made it come true.

I have a dream and a vision for everyone out there. Use this book and manual to become the best YOU can be. Take care and use my words to live your dreams forever and a day.

David John W. StClair

ACKNOWLEDGMENTS

Many thanks and appreciation go out to Dr. Richard Bandler, whom I consider to be the greatest "Lion King" of change and Robert Dilts who inspired me to take his groundbreaking studies as a blueprint for my work. Richard Bandler and Robert Dilts created many outstanding books and products and I highly recommend that you check them out.

Special gratitude goes out to Bettina Smart for an outrageous proof reading!

Genius Mindset Walt Disney

Live your dreams and manifest visions in your reality

Preface and Introduction

Which vision do you want to manifest during the next week?

Some time ago Jim came to me asking for a coaching session as he so urgently craved to change his life into a wonderful and abundant one. I always consider it to be an amazing gift to experience during my coaching work that we special and unique human beings deep inside know where we long to be.

My grandpa once said "you only have the perception and awareness of a problem because you already have the proper solution deep inside yourself waiting to be unleashed!"

Grandpa was a wise man with a bunch of very practical life experiences and I guess a lot of credit goes out to him for letting me become such an effective solution and result oriented coach.

Jim was a very gifted creative person wishing to be a successful online entrepreneur.
His "only" problem was that "my ideas and visions shortly after I feel excited about them always fall apart and I don't give attention to them anymore!"

Already foreseeing what he might reply, I wanted to know if he had an idea why his visions fell apart so quickly?

"Well I have that voice in my mind giving me orders in a very convincing tone: "Back off from that crazy dream as an average guy like you won't ever make it anyway!" That voice scares me and I feel paralyzed for hours so I stopped having dreams a long time ago. I decide to better be realistic instead and concentrate on what I have, like my job as a bartender. This income nearly covers all the costs but why dream at all?"

If Walt Disney would have asked himself the same question Disneyland and Ducksburg would have faded away in a minute. What never faded away was the dream of my stepson to go on an adventurous journey with some friends in a caravan. Dan my stepson was excited that he talked about his vision to be the "Journey of my lifetime". During dinner he even talked about the places they wanted to visit.

Sometimes when you unleash all of the power for a dream it becomes more and more vibrant and alive until the energies are so powerful and seductive that you can't resist to just go for it.

When I asked him whether he had calculated how much money he needed to take with him he replied "no but I can think about that later anytime soon".

I was happy to meet his friend Tony the other day. Tony was a very loyal friend to Dan, as well as smart and flexible in his thinking.

Tony shared the excitement with Dan about the journey completely, but there was a main difference between the two.

The time I met Tony he carried a little pile of notes with him. His explanation impressed me very much: "You know Dan is dreaming so much about this that I am thinking nearly day and night what needs to be done to make this great journey happen – what steps do we have to take in the appropriate sequence and order to let this dream come true.

That's why I use Google so much to find the best places for fishing in the area we want to travel to as well as of course looking for a gorgeous caravan to rent and so much more we need to plan and think about. I want to concrete as much as I can to make this the journey of our lifetime!
My dad calls me the man for the action plan and I consider this to be a great compliment, don't you think?"

Indeed a compliment and a well-earned one. I guess you also know these feelings when you plan precisely, enjoying that this ability is an utterly effective tool for achieving goals.

The next day my stepson came home after having some fun with "da crew" and I instantly knew that something must have happened that bothered him. "What does your facial expression want to tell me son?" I asked with anticipation.

"Well Dad I have been hit by the "How hammer" today." "A how hammer? What do you mean by that?"

Richard's mum came home earlier from her work and as Richard is the third of the ultimate journey crew she took us aside and fired the "how hammer" straight into our ears.

"How will you guys come up with the needed money for such a long journey? How will we as parents find out if everything is fine? How will you guys take care of everything and not forget some most important things like enough clothes, emergency medical supply if anyone gets hurt – there are so many things that could go wrong here."

Dan really seemed a bit disappointed, and I realized the right idea to cheer him up was forming inside me: "Do you know what? Why don't you listen to some great music that will support you to dream about this great journey and come up with a series of solutions so that you will be able to fire back the "explanation hammer" at her?

Just relax and have an amazing vision where all of her "hows" are answered with the most appropriate solutions as you might experience that the excellent feelings double doing this – yes they even can multiply as the vision becomes even stronger and more and more magnetic finding perfect solutions experiencing that everything will work out even better than you could have imagined before?"

The look on his face showed sudden awareness as if it exploded in sun and pleasure. I obviously hit the right spot, I heard him say: "Thank you dad you simply rock!"

Rocks mostly are solid but thinking patterns can change and new effective strategies can be incorporated smoothly just following the steps needed to apply master mindsets and strategies even at an unconscious level with unconscious competence.

Disney founded the most amazing entertainment industry and we definitely remember the fun we might have had following the inhabitants of Ducksburg or the smile he put on our faces with Pinocchio, Bambi, Jungle Book and so much more.

You now might sit here reading these lines and reliving some of these excellent memories as it becomes very obvious why the strategies of billionaires and geniuses will change your life profoundly enriching all areas completely.

Making these mindsets and strategies "your own" with all needed NLP modeling tools, powerful exercises to incorporate knowledge with all senses will be an excellent decision, you can also enjoy looking back from your brilliant future already now that you are about to emerge out of the realm of infinite possibilities.

My expert guidance will assist you to apply this magic generalized in every area of your life as I let you unleash your inner genius and potential unfolding a life where solving problems, turning visions into action and manifesting dreams is just a normal ingredient for your most wonderful life evolving into a miracle you even did not dare to dream about half an hour ago.

Exercises, webinars, live training, audio files and video sequences will build the most amazing package for you on your fulfilling journey to live an enriched and enhanced life from now on with the mindsets and strategies billionaire and genius style .
(Valid for online course subscribers only!)

I will monitor your progress at the forum where you also will feel comforted remembering the opportunity to personally interact with me helping you to boost occasionally whenever you need assistance along the way during your subscription.

There once was a time where you could not write and writing with all these letters and strange new forms felt like something too difficult and impossible to master.....but......wasn't it an amazing day when you learned how to write your name for the first time?

No matter whether it was with your right hand or your left hand it was right that it sometimes was left to do new things at various locations, feeling more and more like an expert.

You might not even remember consciously yet that knowledge will stay profoundly with you when it's in the muscle.

You would have been able to write your name in the sand with a foot after you had written it for the first time with your hand, because your neurology is capable of generalizing learning.

That exactly describes what I will take care of. You will be able to apply the Disney mindset for ultimate creativity, effective problem solving and turning visions into action not only in your business life but also when it comes to relationships, wealth planning, health, fitness and whatever you might think of immediately.

Makes it revolutionarily useful doesn't it?

I am very confident that you will be ahead of the competition when it comes to the question: "How much pleasure can you stand?" applying these mindsets in your daily life.

Feel free to answer the question with your commitment and actions, your determination and the will to embrace all excellent feelings that already are sent your way from the post office of destiny and abundance as you follow and apply what is about to come right now.

I bet Jim, after having asked for a coaching session, would have wished to have attended this program because he would have been proud of himself that it can be easy to manifest visions and dreams into pleasure and peace of mind.

After a few sessions I got a call from Jim telling me that he was so happy to be able to dream, to plan and to enjoy the Disney mindset to create the life he always wanted.

Let this be the perfect opening as I feel we are ready to go take the pedal to the metal entering your highway to excellence – right now.

Many thanks for subscribing – here we go – have fun with me as your ultimate master mind and coach by your side. To your success and abundance.

David John W. StClair

FOUNDATION

ANCHORING

You know it from so many experiences in your life. Suddenly you hear a special song and your mood changes into excellent positive feelings, excitement, exhilaration and pure fun.

Maybe a few days ago there was a fragrance that put a smile on your face or boosted your confidence unfolding significant great energies associated with this olfactory input. There are zillions of examples I could write about, but without my help you are an expert in remembering top experiences of your life and all those wonderful energies and feelings associated with it.

"What is an anchor?" you might ask.

An anchor is a stimulus ----> response mechanism, where you suddenly face a certain stimulus and always the same response takes place.

We will use this powerful tool to enable you to take control and become the director and producer of the best script of your life you can imagine.

It's a wonderful fact that we all have the ability to remember and to forget. I bet you will not be able to recall what you ate 4 years and 12 days ago or what you wore this day?

In the same way it is not important now whether you choose to forget to remember or to remember forgetting what once stood in your way to let the most amazing visions unfold for you to see manifesting in your life as your unconscious already is setting up many ideas how you will use anchors as magical tools to assist you in incorporating the Disney mindset more and more like an expert.

Anchors use your neurology to recall the anchored state like a reflex, as you now begin to take control imagining what kind of energies and feelings you might use in your daily life to enhance it significantly

I ask you to remember a time when you were utterly curios in the most positive way. Maybe you waited the whole day to unwrap the birthday or Christmas present and you just knew that it was that special gift you had been waiting for.

Yes you're doing great – dive deeper into the situation enjoying all great feelings associated with it.

Did you imagine having fun with the present at various places and with different friends? What is there to be seen as you relive this special situation of positive curiosity? What do you see there?

Which sounds and feelings are the "kicker" that make this situation a pure well of magic curiosity? Add the sounds and feelings as I ask your unconscious now to double the feeling of curiosity in a very pleasant way.

As you achieve the peak of your curiosity now choose an appropriate word for this situation containing a condensed energy of this special "C – tuation".

Perfect – would you have thought that all is fine and you are learning well as we add another amplifier for you to enjoy?

Take your thumb and index finger and press them tightly together as you dive deeply into the peak of these "C" feelings. Press thumb and index finger together tightly for a moment.

Now I ask your unconscious to let you access that special state of curiosity easily anytime you are in contact with our program – may it be reading this manual, following a webinar, live online training or enjoying the amazing community *your unconscious now* will take care that you access your most intense state of curiosity any time you are in contact with our excellent program to enjoy multiple benefits and enhancements for your pleasurably unfolding life.

Congratulations! You just learned effective anchoring without consciously noticing that this would happen. Excellent!

You will experience that I add more and more state of the art modules to let you integrate and learn with fun and satisfaction.

Let's dive deeper into the mindset of Walt Disney to let you become an expert in the fields of creativity, effective problem solving and turning visions into actions and reality.

The three Stages of Creativity
Walt Disney Mindset

The Dreamer

Strategies can be explained as a sequence of steps involving our five senses as a foundation to experience and perceive our world.

First we have visual (all we see – defined as "V"), auditory (all we hear defined as "A"), everything related to feelings called kinesthetic (defined as "K"), the olfactory channel involving everything we smell (defined as "O") and all we taste (gustatory defined as "G")

Mostly the first three senses are the most important and dominant ones.

Walt Disney is reborn inside the brain of many highly successful people all over the world. And the especially motivating factor that you are connecting the powerful ability of innovative creativity with successful business can carry you through the next pages as your thumb and index finger know what to do.

Disney also knew what to do and applied naturally when it came to dream. Disney produced so many features and hours of entertainment that to name them alone would fill a book.

The tools of NLP enable you to see the steps Disney applied in his mind to incorporate them as if they were yours right from the beginning. Seeing, hearing and feeling combined in a certain sequence form the foundation of true creativity.

One key tool was the ability to perceive in different perceptual positions.

You might ask yourself right now if he only would tell me more please.

One of Disney's animators is quoted to have said "There were actually three different Walts: The dreamer, the realist and the spoiler. You never knew which one was coming to your meeting."

(Robert B. Dilts: *Strategius of Genius. Volume I: Aristotle, Sherlock Holmes, Walt Disney, Wolfgang Amadeus Mozart.* Meta Publications, Capitalo (California/USA) 1994, ISBN 0-916990-32-X.)

There you have the secret of excellent creativity laid out seductively on the table. Teamwork of these three different states forms the ultimate power for the creative process.

A pure dreamer will not be able to turn visions into actions and results without the realist. Dreamer and critic alone will be trapped in eternal conflict as if being in perpetual motion without result.

Realist and dreamer together might be able to produce results but as you read on you definitely won't settle for anything less being with me here than for high quality and the pure essence of top - notch results – so this definitely needs the critic as inspiring element.

We will look at this very useful filter expert for creativity and refinement later.

Looking at Disney's body posture and gestures during his dreamer state he is described as having lowered one eye brow, squinting his eyes, letting his jaw drop staring fixedly at some point in space, holding this attitude for several moments. Nobody would have been able to break this state. (Quote from Robert B.

Dilts: *Strategius of Genius. Volume I: Aristotle, Sherlock Holmes, Walt Disney, Wolfgang Amadeus Mozart*. Meta Publications, Capitalo (California/USA) 1994, ISBN 0-916990-32-X.)

The sentence "knowledge is nothing until it is in the muscle" spontaneously comes to mind. His whole neurology was committed and involved in the process making it possible to access this strategy and dreamer state easily when needed.

According to NLP looking up to the right is related to constructing or fantasizing visual images (**V**).

Exercise one

Creating knowledge of the muscles

1) Find the very special place in your office and/or home that will be your "dreamer" paradise from now on. A place where you feel best visualizing, fantasizing, just an excellent place for your own personal superhero turbo charged dreaming style.

2) Let something come to mind you want to manifest or visualize.

3) Adopt the formerly described body position (looking up to the right, lower one eye brow, squint your eyes, let your jaw drop and stare fixedly at some point in space. Hold this attitude for several moments).

Breathe in a most supporting way as you simply let go and purely follow your imagination as your unconscious assists you in having a wonderful vision about the dream you want to manifest in your life.
Adopt the attitude that here and now possibilities are endless, any limitation that blocked you from visualizing perfectly effectively has melted like ice in the sun as you enjoy becoming an expert of visualization.

4) Enjoy as you find the perfect most appropriate word for your dreamer state.

5) Continue to see the vision unfold as you allow all related positive feelings to enter you like a long desired extra positive surprise.

6) Return into the present, refreshed, curious and excited that this great start was only the beginning.

Congratulations! *You just earned your first grade A as a super MoV (Master of Visualization)*

Allow yourself to be proud – I wonder whether you knew from the beginning that you would perform so excellently following these words and instructions as if you had waited for them so long?

That's right!

Are you ready to move on to the next level?

As you have advanced so easily you might now take a break, shake your body a bit, enjoy a glass of delicious water or some

fruit or just continue to follow me at your own perfect rate and speed as your unconscious will integrate all learning smoothly.

And like an expert during your wonderfully refreshing and nurturing sleep assisting you apply the exercise at least three days in a row to let the knowledge ingrain deeply in your muscles with ease.

Perfect, so let's level up to the next stage *MoV expert.*

Foundation to enhance the Dreamer

NLP submodalities

Full credit for developing the concept of submodalities goes to Dr. Richard Bandler, co - creator and for me the ultimate wizard of NLP. It was a pure pleasure to assist as a trainer during Richard's trainings and seminars in Germany for several years.

Richard Bandler is that massively dedicated to making the life of every person he meets better and full of quality that I am proud to have learned so much directly from Richard and I will now pass on to you some secrets to let you learn from the best.

Like me you can easily re enter your state of curiosity to add the next power module to your inner creativity machine already warming up again to your pleasure and success.

What are submodalities?

(Quoted from: http://en.wikipedia.org/wiki/Submodalities) NLP asserts that far from being arbitrary or unimportant, these submodalities often perform a functional role, as a means by which emotions, related memories, felt-sense perceptions such as "importance" etc. are presented to our consciousness by the unconscious mind, along with thoughts or memories.

The metaphor of "distancing oneself" is taken quite literally, the mental representation of something unimportant is "farther away" than something important.

NLP asserts that amongst the many possible submodalities, there often will be a handful of so called *"critical"* submodalities which can functionally effect large-scale change, which differs from person to person and can be identified by observation and inquiry.

NLP states that a change within these critical submodalities will often correlate with a nearly immediate subjective change in the emotion or other felt sense with which a mental impression presents itself.

Submodalities are therefore seen in NLP as something offering a valuable therapeutic insight (or metaphor) and potential working methods into how the human mind organizes internally and subjectively 'views' events.

Richard Bandler as developer and creator of this concept stated that our ability to change the way we feel depends on our ability to change and alter these submodalities.

These are great news! Instead of being a victim of circumstances in the here and now it unleashes the enormous power that you are capable of changing situations, uncomfy feelings and your internal states by altering or changing your perception using the gorgeous toolbox of submodalities.

These aspects will form a gorgeous foundation for the next modules letting you evolve into an expert more and more!

So let's move on.

Everything we do inside our mind and body can be described in terms of things we see, hear, feel, smell and taste.

In NLP the five senses that comprise our sensory input channels are also known as modalities.

The richness and diversity of experience available to us as human beings demands that our sensory input channels support a fine level of distinction or granularity, and thus the modalities are made up of smaller sub components known as submodalities.

Any experience that we have in life is going to have a certain set of submodalities and the order, sequence and properties of those submodalities are the way in which we encode that particular experience as we add it to our internal map of reality.

Changing an experience in our internal map can be easily achieved by simply changing the submodalities of the experience to recode it.

For example, we can take something we dislike and change it into something we like by:

Eliciting the submodalities of the thing we dislike (substance A), eliciting the submodalities of something that we like (substance B), recoding our experience of substance A by mapping onto it the submodalities of substance B. Simple, elegant and very useful.

We will dive deeper into this concept and absolutely gorgeous tool with the next parts. Unleashing the "giant" called submodalities will let you change beliefs, enhance the dreamer in extraordinary ways letting you implement the strategy so easily that you might even not remember when you started to turn a very important vision into action reading this amazing program as you apply it successfully in your daily life.

There are way too many options to be tried out to mention – a fact that makes me happy as you are a freshly honored MoV master and already will begin to let visions unfold how to use all this effectively and pleasantly.

Exercise – Submodality Elicitation

As mentioned above elicitation means to write down and find out the submodalities which mainly trigger your feelings about a certain experience as your unconscious will apply and learn with unconscious competence. Soon you also might let your brain enjoy the following list of submodalities as a set of tools to play with.

List of submodalities

Here is a list of NLP submodalities. When finding out your blueprint, use this list as a guide.

Visual

Color: Is it in color or black & white? Are the colors vivid or washed out? Is it full color spectrum?

Brightness: Is it brighter or darker than normal? What is the degree of brightness?

Contrast: Is it high contrast or low contrast?

Focus: Is the image sharp or fuzzy?

Texture: Is the texture of the image smooth or rough?

Detail: Are there foreground and background details? Do you see the details as part of a whole or do you have to shift focus to see them?

Size: How big is the image? (Check specific size)

Distance: How far away is the image? (Be specific)

Shape: What is the shape of the picture? Square, round, rectangular?

Border: Is there a border to the image? Does the border have a color? How thick is it?

Location: Where is the image located in space?

Movement: Is it a movie or still picture? How fast is the movement, faster or slower than normal? Is the image stable? What direction does the image move to?

Association/Disassociation: Do you see yourself or do you see the event as if you were there?

Perspective: From what perspective do you see it? (For disassociated) do you see yourself from front, back, left or right?

Proportion: Are the sizes of the things in the image in proportion to one another? Are they larger or smaller than life?

Dimension: Is the image 3D or flat?

Singular/Plural: Do you see one image or more than one? Do you see them together or one after the other?

Auditory

Location: Where does the sound originate? Do you hear it from inside or outside?

Pitch: High or low pitched? Higher or lower than normal?
Tone: What is the tone?

Melody: Is it monotone or melodic?

Volume: How loud is it?

Tempo: Fast or slow?

Rhythm: Does it have a beat?

Mono/Stereo: Do you hear it on one side or both sides?

Kinesthetic

Intensity: How strong is the sensation?

Quality: How would you describe it? Tingling, warm, cold, relaxed, tense?

Location: Where do you feel it in your body?

Movement: Is there movement in the sensation? Is the movement continuous or does it come in waves?

Direction: Where does the sensation start? Where does it move to? How (in what direction) does it move?

Speed: Is it a slow progression or does it move in a rush?

Looking at the list of submodalities you can see that there are many options to be tried when it comes to visualization. During an NLP trainers training I did in the 90ties we made a student get rid of his allergy related to apples within 10 minutes using submodalities.

Our brain codes experiences in certain sets of chemicals and molecules. Experiencing the same stimulus means unleashing the same set of molecules, having the same feelings, experiencing the same set of options in terms of behavior.

Submodalities are a powerful tool to widen the range of options in every area of your life.

The following examples will show you a bunch of perspectives you will use in your every day life letting your dreams come true applying the Disney strategy for extraordinary creativity and phenomenal creative problem solving.

I once had a client with very low self esteem in his business life. Whenever he had to see his boss to report how things are going (and this was at least twice a week, he felt like a mouse in front of a hungry lion. This caused a very stressful environment for him and also for his family.

He asked for advice and help and this is what the change with the help of submodalities did for him within 20 minutes (problem solved!)

First was the elicitation phase to find out what exactly caused the stress in his mind thinking about a meeting with his boss? He told that the scene was dim and dark except the region of the desk where his boss was sitting looked like being lit up by a giant series of spotlights.

The eyes of his boss would be 5 times larger than in real life staring at him ferociously. He also saw his boss only from head to neck.

I advised him to use submodalities like changing brightness by letting the sun shine through the whole room, making the eyes of his boss smaller, seeing him as a whole person, adding a sound of confidence to the scene to make him feel better, expanding the feeling of being capable in his body, painting the wall in friendly colors and adding an inner dialogue to the scene: "I am self confident, capable, feeling relaxed and focused in every meeting with my boss."

I asked him what could enhance the situation to make him feel even more excellent. He smiled and said: "If my boss wore a t-shirt with a smiley on it saying "love ya buddy"!"

I then instructed his unconscious mind to imagine his boss wearing the same shirt he was imagining in his mind every time it would be helpful during a meeting and no matter what he would be wearing in reality to stay in this inner resource state.
Three days later he called me: "Wow, this was an amazing meeting.

I was so focused, my breathing had changed and my hands had been warm as I was relaxed all time.

The best thing was that I perceived his eyes and the room light the way we had worked it out.

The "kicker" was his smiley shirt though! I was completely stunned when my boss told me: "This was the best report ever - you seemed less tense and more centered - please stay this way as I have appreciated your work for a long time!"

As a MoV you already might have some creative and amazing ideas how to use these powerful tools to make your dreams come true.

Let's give your new knowledge a chance to ingrain even deeper with the next exercise.

Upgrade module – Enhancing the Dreamer

1) Take care that nothing can disturb you for the next minutes and also turn your phone off during the exercise. Yes, there is a reason to feel pleasure because we add a new portion of unconscious competence to your skill set!

2) Go back to your anchored dreamer location, pick a vision – a dream you want to make come true soon.

3) Adjust your body posture the way you already learned – remember with eyes looking up....

4) Dive deep into your vision/dream you want to make come true soon.

• Test the list of submodalities and use the ones that make the dream/vision magnetically so attractive in a way that you feel how it clicks and you are so irresistibly connected to it that the joy that your unconscious mind will assist you beyond belief to move towards that vision honestly and with action right away after you have learned the other elements of the strategy, you will notice how extraordinary enhancement spreads throughout this process and every vision you fire up with your set of success and

Abundance tools incorporated skillfully and with that special magic that everything will be all right now.

6) Maybe a choir of 1000 motivating voices cheering you up and telling you "Go for it!", brighten up colors, make it a colorful orgy and try whatever works for you, turn it into 3 dimensional all around experience and as I ask your unconscious to make this experience 10 times more intense letting your dreamer learn on

an ongoing basis you don't even have to know consciously yet how perfectly you walk your path towards mastery right here.

7) As you see the vision let yourself be surprised how easily you will get a feeling to „*understand*" *your vision /dream* as if feeling and seeing overlap as you gain a new *understanding and insight*. Enjoy this process as your unconscious supports you in the best expert imaginable way to enhance the "kicker" submodalities even more. Participating in our webinars, live trainings or radio shows will also help you to incorporate the material as if you were genetically born as a super hero of creativity and creative problem solving

•   Have fun with your progress and allow yourself to be proud of yourself as you are doing extraordinary great. Think of something you can give yourself after that exercise as a gratification – a special fruit juice, some minutes walking in nature or listening with complete awareness to your favorite music feeling what you hear from within lifting you up.

•   Take a break and continue later with our amazing program.

Tadaa – special congratulations as you have added the new upgrade module to your path of mastery. Isn't it an amazing pleasure to ride the highway to excellence learning to think as a true genius? You are doing great and deserve a short break – see you soon with our next level training.

As both minds are integrating and incorporating your progress we have seen that Disney with his dreamer applied something we call lateral thinking and the overlapping of different representational systems.
V (constructed pictures) – K (feelings) and what we will add now: Movement

Movement does not only relate to the formerly mentioned synesthesia but also to a huge improvement of the dreamer upgrade you are going to add now.

As pictures and feelings enabled Disney to see the „big picture" of the vision, how things would be connected to each other until everything made „perfect sense" he also slipped into the body of the characters.
The story goes that every time he gave his voice to one oft the characters he exactly made the same movements/body postures the character was performing to *be completely "in the flow"* acting from the inside. This gave existential breath of life to his animations and successful movies.

There once was a knock at my door. Waiting for a positive surprise and a chance to learn from the person knocking, no matter who it might be, there is always a chance to enjoy and learn from another unique being like you, me and everybody, I opened the door with curiosity.

It was Nancy, a woman who had talked with me two days before, to enjoy some coaching craving to settle an argument with a colleague at work.

I immediately demonstrated my utter trust in her abilities to achieve her desired outcome with all my options like voice, body posture, targeted use of power sentences and specifically structured communication.

This instantly let her *breathe deeply then.* She did not even think about the benefits of experiencing different positions in learning how to solve problems effectively as *the brain generalizes new learning* just like you do as you read on.

First step was that I invited her to experience that this situation and even the connected and related pattern would never be the same after a few minutes for everybody involved here.

„Nancy, as you and me will have some fun changing this resourcefully for you and with light speed, please imagine the situation and step into it for the last time as you had experienced it from the view of tomorrow. How do you feel in that situation?"

„Well David John, I feel like a victim, helpless and inferior. I am breathing fast and feel tension in my stomach and nearly could throw up. As if I am guilty and worth less."

Her shoulders had dropped, her breath rate had sped up and her whole facial expression and physiology showed me that she experienced a completely stressful situation.

„Ok Nancy, thanks a lot for having experienced this situation for the last time ever like you have just now. Please change position with me and do us a favor and dance on one foot as you sing your most favorite child tune."

She looked at me as if I had gone nuts but in our first talk we had already discussed that problems could not be solved at the same level they originated, so thinking out of the box and applying new effective methods combined with fun excited her pleasantly from the beginning.

Nancy started to hop on one foot singing „I'm A Moose With A Cowlick". A few seconds later she was rolling on the floor laughing nearly peeing in her pants out of fun.

Amazing Nancy, that's what learning is all about.

We learn most effectively in extraordinary excellent states and as you learn most powerful tools for state management, your always assisting unconsciousness already has begun to generalize.

Follow me to the movie theater I call "change with pleasure and ease island" where I have two chairs.

Take a seat Nancy and let's have fun watching a movie from a distance without unpleasant feelings." We sat down as I guided her further.

"Now Nancy as you enter this slightly pleasant learning relaxation, imagine seeing you and me watching a Nancy over there (as I pointed towards the location she had experienced the situation of conflict for the last time) and this Nancy over there watches Nancy acting in the situation, which already is about to change.

Let her look at Nancy's communication partner. Let her see how he behaves, his gestures, body posture, breathing and the characteristics of his communication.

What can she tell us as new important insight from over there?"

"Wow he has his arms crossed before his chest, feet crossed, hands tremble, high pitched voice and it seems as if he is looking for a door to escape."

"Great insight Nancy – what would he need to enjoy this situation as a resourceful discussion with you? Let Nancy over there come up with some gorgeous effective ideas now!"

"She tells me that he is full of pressure from his boss and that he somehow feels trapped in a cage built of expectations and fear to lose the job. She tells me that he needs self confidence and the feeling that Nancy over there also intends to experience this conversation as pleasant and solution oriented."

"Wonderful Nancy – please kindly ask that Nancy over there to give him over there everything he needs in the shape of helpful energies, maybe in a certain color, a wizard's spell that all will be fine and that he will be extremely influenced in a positive way, noticing that Nancy there in the distance is learning to change this situation and all involved patterns effectively and completely for the best.

Let her notice how his body posture changes, his behavior is altered in a way that Nancy in the distance in this communication enjoys the changes resourcefully as I thank her unconscious mind for its perfect assistance. Let her please tell you when his healing is finished and everything has been integrated completely."

Nancy beside me sitting in the "movie chair" enjoyed the process with a look on her face that mirrored her fascination. She was breathing relaxed as I anchored this state to help her later with it if needed.

"As the other Nancy watching the two over there is such a master of change, let her now tell you what Nancy in this situation would need to feel exclusively resourceful and amazing in that communication."

After a few seconds of interaction with "Master Nancy" she took a deep and even more relaxing breath. I felt a huge wave of inspiring insight building up in her.

"That is what I call amazing! Nancy tells me that the other Nancy over there needs something I'd call basic trust in life and in herself, self confidence and that she quits depending on appreciation from the outside – she needs to appreciate herself first." "I'm so excited to experience this, can I please tell her to give Nancy in the communication over there all she needs?"

"Of course as your unconscious has already told you that it takes care responsively that you apply the amazing progress and learning on various levels in your daily life from now on becoming an expert, exchanging the former victim role with the new Nancy, driving her own bus as she uses her brain for true change!"

"She gives her basic trust in life in her favorite color, self confidence supported by friends cheering her up and a banner on the walls saying: "You simply rock Nance!" and a chewing gum to let her incorporate and chew self acceptance and appreciation.

I never would have thought that Nancy can be so creative – that is the most amazing experience I had in a long time!"

"All right now – please let "Master Nancy" take all the time she needs to give Nancy over there in the situation all resources she needs including a bonus from me that includes the following:

I hereby let my condensed and special long lasting change containing magical dust rain upon her and this dust also shines over her whole future throughout the years and decades to come.

Nancy is a self regulating and self organizing being walking her path of infinite creativity and she is amazing in solving problems properly incorporating all of this phenomenal knowledge.

Learning "Master Nancy Style" will stay with her for the rest of her long, happy and healthy life now as *your unconscious* supports you to let Nancy over there *integrate everything so perfectly* that you don't even have to notice yet how much impact this will have on her life consistently evolving during her journey on her individual highway to excellence."

"Nancy looked as if she was glowing from within and she definitely deserved it as she once again within your infinite realm of positive changes has proven that humans can change rapidly long lastingly with extraordinary fun trusting their unconscious as magical power is unleashed from the inside out."

Nancy looked at me as if returning from the pleasure ride of her life.

"Done, David John, Nancy over there feels completely satisfied seeing how intensely Nancy in the situation over there has changed.

Her body posture is so exciting. She stands straight with her arms relaxed at both sides, looking encouraged and friendly into the eyes of her communication partner, appreciating his input, listening actively with understanding and anticipation motivating him to continue with his opinion and perception of the topic.

"What is the next step? I feel that something is still missing."

"Again you prove yourself to be a new expert of excellence, Nancy. Next is that I invite you to stand up with me leaving this movie chair maybe with an attitude of gratitude.

Prepare yourself to experience me revealing a secret to you – a very important secret. I just got a message from your second foot. It also wants to hop to let you sing the tune again as you rock on with the child tune one more time."

Nancy burst out with laughter and began to sing instantly until she was rolling on the floor laughing like she did before.

This time it was even more natural coming from deep within, presenting laughter combined with a celebration of the moment – a celebration of relief.

"Well Nancy the best dancer claims the prize and the winner is YOU!" With a touch on her shoulder and a snap with my fingers I anchored this great feeling for her utilizing various representational systems – remember anchoring and synesthesia?

"All right Nancy – let's add what you considered to be missing.

Time to integrate the information and learning Nancy over there at her special spectator position experienced as inspiration. Go there and incorporate this version of your Self easily into your personality as your unconscious assists expert style that all learning she experienced will also be yours from now on as you become again the whole person Nancy with all knowledge, experiences and insight she learned before.

Everything experienced and learned is now *becoming your own* as you also integrate the fact to use and apply different positions every time you feel the need to learn and unfold your inner genius for solving problems, improving your daily life and encounters with people and infinite more options you already might have in mind right now.

Yes you are doing great!

(Nancy is breathing deeply, smiling and looking as if something very significantly and important is happening deep inside her). Give me a sign with your right hand when the change is integrated completely (she smiles and waves).

Thank you Nancy that was sensational! You were sensational! Now let's add some upgrade – please travel into the future with your imagination experiencing the next talk with this guy as you feel, see and hear how things changed the other day as you learned so much using different positions… more and more light-speed like…. riding on the waves of trance and change now.

Experience the change out of your own eyes as you acquire new knowledge. You realize that there already have been many moments and situations where you applied this new insight and learning like an expert and with unconscious competence. It has been completely amazing to experience different perceptual positions as you solved problems smoothly, hasn't it?"

"Oh yes, David John, that is the most amazing experience I had in years if not in decades. I am in control now and I can change my life using the rapidly unleashed power out of my inner center of creativity and imagination!

Thank you so much.

I already feel, how my brain makes lists where and with whom I want to apply this, but the process seems to run on autopilot as I feel myself doing what we did here effortlessly and with amazement and fun!"

"Gorgeous Nancy – feel free to come back anytime to learn some more techniques for other issues whenever you might feel that assistance for your unique inner evolution is appropriate."

"Of course David John, I already have something in mind, but I want to have fun applying this amazing position thing for a while – have a great day!"

"You too Nancy and enjoy the ride!"

Exercise Perceptual Positions and Disney

1) Repeat the exercise contacting your vision, diving into it with dreamer physiology and gestures as well as diving deeply into the vision with submodality enhancement. Of course at your anchored dreamer location that you already have with you in your mind wherever you go!

2) Now step into the vision in your mind and melt with the version of your Self in this vision.

3) Like Disney once said "every action should be based on what the character represents," (Quote: notice exactly what you represent in your vision. What are the beliefs and values you live in this vision?

4) Give in to your trust in your unconscious assistance and let your unconscious tell you in your dreams a variety of insight and input, what you represent in this vision, what values you embody and what you stand for in your desired vision/dream. How do these values and beliefs affect your gestures and body posture?

•   Enjoy a break or a refreshing sleep, where you might try scenes in which you experience yourself acting the way you experienced yourself in your vision applying this exercise.

This way you enrich your Self in a way that enhances your set of behavior and options. This sharpens your focus on your vision and dream.

Have fun!

Wow, time for a toast! You just mastered another upgrade on your highway to excellence and on your path to thinking like a genius. I am completely impressed how amazing you follow all these exercises with your complete commitment to apply learning in your every day life.

I also sense that you feel more and more excited and competent as your curiosity increases even more.

Summary Dreamer

Having mastered the first module definitely feels gorgeous, Doesn't it? Let me once more express my joy that you did so well following me along in this amazing program.

Remember to unfold the dreamer Disney style means to let your imagination run wild, completely free, generate ideas, visions and dreams without judging them – just creativity unleashed at your anchored dreamer location or visiting your dreamer location in your mind.

Enhance the state, your dream/vision with submodalities and keep perceptual positions in mind.

Practice, practice, practice and have fun with your expert ability to generate ideas, solutions and sets of various options – no matter if it's about problem solving or manifesting dreams and visions first hand applying your knowledge as if it were with you from the beginning!

Most of all: Have fun with your mastery! How much pleasure can you stand realizing that this course helps you profoundly to feel good for no reason :)

It definitely will be useful to apply the given exercises frequently to let them easily become a natural set of behavior automatically whenever you need assistance from the dreamer.

Genius Mindset Walt Disney
Module

The Realist

Isn't it absolutely amazing to make such progress as you enjoy each and every step of your mastery?

Perfect – you deserve to be proud! You are definitely doing an excellent job here.

Let's continue and add extra power to this genius strategy and mindset becoming more and more important in your life. Now I will deliver more fun, because I will provide you with an intense feeling of competence and energy to manifest your visions and dreams precisely further into reality.

Disney was not only a master when it came to have visions of infinite power and creativity – his second core ability was to turn dreams and visions into reality.

(Quote: Robert B. Dilts: *Strategius of Genius. Volume I: Aristotle, Sherlock Holmes, Walt Disney, Wolfgang Amadeus Mozart*. Meta Publications, Capitalo (California/USA) 1994, ISBN 0-916990-32-X.)

"Dreams must have a solid foundation to express sincerity. Having a vision or a dream in the realist stage means to study it from every angle and not just superficially.

To be truly inventive you need an excellently established feedback loop between the dreamer and the realist.

The key strategy is here the ability to chunk the vision/dream down to tangible and manageable pieces that can be turned into reality.

Disney is considered to be the inventor of a process called story-boarding.

Awesome – ready to make it the "real thing?"

Let's *go for it!*

Exercise

Finding and anchoring the realist state

Remember already being an expert in anchoring? In particular we are talking about utilizing your neurology to create a positive and compelling stimulus-response matrix.

The following exercise will enable you to enter the realist state according to your free will to drive dreams and visions magnetically towards manifestation.

1) Find a place and location that will be perfectly associated with being a realist. Disney had a room with white walls and the heat turned up stating that hard work and sweat would be closely connected.

2) Sit there in a way that you will be able to plan and write things down.

• Remember a time where you could plan excellently, where it was very easy to sort things out and structure them in order so you could get them done smoothly.

4) Dive deeply into this experience, seeing through your own eyes what there is to see, what do you hear, feel, smell or taste that makes the situation so real, so efficient?

5) Enhance the situation applying your knowledge about submodalities. Boost this experience in a way that you are the master planner, the world champ of being able to chop things up

into manageable pieces to transform a vision into determined action.

6) As your unconsciousness doubles the feelings clearly each 5 breaths enjoy its assistance finding an appropriate word for this state.

7) After you have found a word, enhance this word with auditory submodalities like Dolby surround sound, choir, echo – whatever increases the impact this word affects on you significantly.

Choose a movement that expresses this *ground breaking realist experience perfectly* as if this moment were condensed in a movement as you say the word.

8) Apply the movement – repeat it three times as you say the word, hearing it also inside with all previous submodality enhancements and enjoy being proud of yourself having mastered the next level on your highway to excellence! Congrats you once again did a gorgeous job here!

Time to celebrate again – be good to yourself. Think about something you can reward yourself to enjoy your ongoing progress. Some nice minutes walking outside, having fun with pleasant fresh air noticing that this could be a symbol for the freshness entering your life more and more intensely as you continue focused on your path to mastery and excellence!

Maybe a wonderful tasting juice reminding you of the fact that life tastes just wonderful if you open up for all these exciting chances around you?

Have fun with it as I prepare the next upgrade for you.

Exercise

Applying the Realist Strategy
Story-Boarding

Remember the story from the beginning about my stepson and the journey of his lifetime?

Ah yes, there was the friend his father called "the man for the action plan!"

You're right, he was carrying notes with him to assist my stepson to let the dream and vision of this amazing journey come true.

A week after my son had been inspired to find the "explanation hammer" by asking his unconscious to dream about solutions for the "how hammer" Richards mum had thrown "into his ears and face", I met Dan and Tony in our living room.

The boys were not only enjoying a fresh fruit salad but were also busy with some papers.

Their faces looked pretty excited, so I approached them with a smile: "Hey guys any news about the journey of your lifetime?"

"Absolutely yes, Mr. StClair," answered Tony, before Dan even had a chance to reply.

"We were at Richard's two days ago and Dan was amazing.

Richards mum just started again to ask all her "how" questions, but Dan stood straight, breathing relaxed and gave her at least 3 great alternatives generating amazing solutions for each and every how she asked. That was way cool!"

"That's great to hear guys. I am confident that you will have a rocking journey. What function do the papers on the desk have? Are these the ones you carried with you when we talked the first time Tony?"

Now it was Dan's turn to answer: "Well Dad, I have told Tony everything about my dreams, visions and all the ideas I have. Tony is our Google master so he regularly looks things up, does exact research and all the results he comes up with give us the excellent feeling that the journey becomes more and more real.

We all have nice jobs and we will throw the money in a box to earn a pile we can use as money for the journey and the events and stuff we want to experience as well as for food and other necessary basics.

Tony compared the whole journey with a tree. You can admire and love the whole tree but what makes the tree so special and unique are the different leaves and branches.

Tony looks from the general towards the specific so that we have milestones and steps let's say breaking the journey down – if I compare that to a movie or book – into scenes or chapters and then even looking closer into certain pages or even sentences.

This is great to look at the plan from weeks down to days. Makes the whole adventure even more exciting for me as I see my vision more and more come down to earth appearing real!"

"That sounds absolutely amazing guys. Go for it as I myself see so many spectacular moments for you that I nearly would think about joining you guys! Before you freak out – I'm just kidding.

I am completely proud how outrageously you handle the whole project – just go for it with curiosity and determination and all will work out even better than you could have planned. Positive surprises are always around the corner."

"Great Dad, thanks for your amazing support. Now Tony let's look at that paper we have for the second week. Have fun Dad we've got to move on."

I was very proud of the guys as I am proud of you already having begun to integrate new info on the realist.

The task of the realist now is two fold. First let's focus on the actual present state:

1) Sit down at your *realist location*, say your trigger word and make the movement as you enter and perform the appropriate realist state.

• Take pieces of paper and write down the actual facts regarding your vision.

3) How much money would be needed and how much is available? What resources do you already have waiting to unleash them manifesting the vision/dream? What resources will be needed? Write it down as precisely as possible. What is the current present state looking at your vision/dream? One column – what is already there? Another column – what do you need?

• Apply your knowledge about perceptual positions and step onto second base – look at the vision out of the eyes of involved people and learn the many input and insight you gain as you do so joyfully.

5) Allow yourself to let pleasure run over in you as you integrate the knowledge that your success will be built on enthusiasm, motivated work and effort, integrity of purpose, confidence in the future and most of all a steady day by day growth and improvement as you feel a magnetic pull towards your manifesting visions and dreams.

6) Take a break, enjoy some fresh air and healthy food or do something that nourishes your mind, body and soul.

7) Continue later with the next upgrade towards mastery on your highway to genius and excellence.

Welcome back!

Isn't it amazing how groundbreaking excitement and curiosity can carry through this excellent mindset program as you remember how easy learning can be out of the right state.
Yes that's so true your thumb and index finger already knew what to do, right?

Most of all remember to feel good for no reason. People make the most excellent and satisfying decisions out of massively positive state of mind. A great way to help you with this is my core transformation CD also available at create space just by clicking the following link.

This CD will enable you to live out of your source and core states like peace of mind or/and oneness. Can you imagine how states like these will additionally support you in manifesting?

Incorporating the realist will add some new skills to your already unfolding conscious and unconscious competence of excellent problem solving and vibrant vision manifestation.
It especially will be the combination of your dreamer and realist that creates powerful impact.

You have worlds to conquer because you are on a journey that lets you dance your song of life in a way that you begin to know what real and true awareness is.

I am well aware that you might have waited for so long to cut the knot that held you back for such a long time and now it already has begun to melt by your own fire.

I am very happy to see you integrate such wisdom.

You right now don't even have to think about the endless positive effects this mindset will have on your bright and shining future.

This reminds me of a former client and now close friend named Alejandro.

Alejandro heard about the journey of the lifetime Dan and his friends would start soon.

I had told him about the great approach the guys were applying. First Alejandro frowned as he also belonged to the crowd in which visions and dreams instantly are destroyed by an inner blocking force or sabotage specialist.

Alejandro wanted to be a successful entrepreneur so we talked about the dreamer.

It was a wonderful experience for him to surrender to his dreamer and unleash all his creativity, visions, dreams and ideas without the slightest bit of any judgment.

We worked it out that one important foundation for creativity is to *unleash ideas completely freely* enjoying the *utter absence of any judgmental attitude* or any prejudice.

This was the first great relief for him to experience how many different ideas he can generate with a *completely free visionary dreamer*. Of course it helped him a lot to having established a certain location anchored to his dreamer first place, but lucky for you, you are already ahead of Alejandro significantly!

Next step for him was to learn from different perceptual positions to look at things from many useful angles, but you also already know that.

Applying the realist, stepping into other involved persons and asking the right questions boosted his creativity and ability to manifest dreams remarkably beyond his wildest expectations.

As you are following us so perfectly you might now witness Alejandro's progress in a way that lets you learn deeply knowing that an important upgrade in your learning already has begun.

"Alejandro, are you ready to learn a little bit magic that will add more expertise to your unfolding mastery?"

"Anytime now David John, you helped me so much that I am already using my magic word for creativity and thumb/index finger works phenomenal too. I am so ready to continue to boost my personal highway to excellence!"

"Awesome Alejandro, best attitude here! Now I want you to find a location where you completely have manifested your dream. A place and space where you are in the middle of success, enjoying the result – your truly fulfilled vision, your dream come true."

Alejandro smiled as his face turned into pure pleasure. He looked as if he had grown wings ready to lift off. He looked towards a certain direction and I encouraged him to go exactly there.

"Great, now as you melt with the future, digest your success with each and every representational system, taste it, feel it, hear it and smell the fragrance of your dream come true.
Use all your knowledge about submodalities and effective enhancement of feelings as I kindly ask *your unconscious* to assist as always utterly and completely.

Now look towards the present, look into a direction where you sense the here and now somewhere in the distance.

Look towards now feeling a strong and indestructible connection build by an amazing magnet.

Feel the energy between the present and your future success space form a stream of blissful and protecting energy, taking care that your vision, your dream only has the chance to manifest brilliantly.

As you look back towards the present, feeling the increasing connection between here and now and your future area of success, your unconscious already has begun to ignite excellent interaction between your destiny and the phenomenal blueprint of abundance shining inside you.

Like a birdie is nurtured by its mother taking care that the wings will unfold to explore worlds and regions yet unknown but not for long until the heart knows *it's time to fly on the wings of faith taking action* to let the path unfold brilliantly.

Now Alejandro as the expertise assistance of *your unconscious* shines from the present all over your future, you are learning that you will be guided by your intuition and the safe knowledge of your inner navigational system working perfectly... adjusted and aligned with your vibrant connection between "dream manifested" and the present over there, you feel the best attitudes and beliefs to let that all happen fall into place smoothly and directly now.

No questioning if you might dream tonight, it does not matter if it will be vibrant dreams, dreams of many manifested dreams and visions or even dreams where you discover later that energies are at work in your life that take care – take care that you will move towards your desired future each day more and more racing on your highway to excellence, abundance unleashed and joy unfolding.

As your unconscious is integrating all this, continue to look back and notice the significant steps that led you there, to the completion and manifestation of your dream.

Go slowly backwards at a rate and speed exactly perfect for you and record internally the significant steps you walked with determination, perseverance and committed action.

This way you learn right now, along the way, here, that you establish a hilarious consulting expert that is YOU out of the eyes of a future YOU. This way you have learned to give yourself excellent advice from future perspectives whenever needed.

Your unconscious will remind you for a little while to support these patterns consciously by going into your future space where problems are creatively solved, dreams came true and visions have manifested powerfully.

Then you go backwards physically and shortly after that in your mind, without needing to do it physically, recording, noticing and incorporating the key actions and factors that led to success.

You are doing so outrageously that I am happy to see you proceed until you have reached the spot related to our present here and now.

As you fully return to the awareness of your present, you feel inside all advice and progress merge with your personality that *your unconscious* can incorporate all tips and advice you collected from the future backwards, *integrating these exceptional great insight into your already existing plan.*

This will work even better than the most efficient catalytic converter, enabling you to speed the manifestation of your dreams and visions up, boosting the result in a way that you will feel more happiness, joy and success than you could have imagined in your wildest dreams.

Now Alejandro, allow yourself to return fully fresh, awaken and vital into the here and now, prepared to enhance your action plan on your successful way to master your degree in future self counseling and manifesting dreams and visions like an expert."

I gave Alejandro enough time to adjust back into the present, enjoying all the newly gained insight integrating and balancing the vision and action plan with this extra special fine tuning and boosting upgrade.

After a while Alejandro realigned fully into the present. It is quite a challenge to describe how Alejandro looked after his "return". His body posture, look and overall appearance had changed completely.

This man was materialized determination and faith. Maybe you also know how it feels to be filled with some extremely positive energy that will nurture you forever and a day? I trust that you will be able to remember and anchor this appropriately?

"Well David John, I am sure you don't mind that I am searching for the right words – this experience was a very special one. I feel completely changed and transformed from the inside out.

Got to go now and perform the next steps to live my dreams celebrating my life. Isn't earth an amazing planet and this life an exhilarating miracle to be lived?"

I smiled at him – he said it all!

Exercise

Unleashing the power of the future – Live your dreams 3.0

Can you imagine how it feels to see a golden key manifest in your hands as you stand in front of the ultimate access of treasure? That's exactly what you are about to experience right now. You have come a long way so far.

Traveling with your MoV degree, *learning the excellence of the realist* and how substantial it is to use story boarding and *mapping the action plan precisely*. This was a great accomplishment after having learned that an unchained dreamer generating ideas without being judged lays a wonderful foundation for manifested abundance and dreams come true.

Now we are getting close to rounding the Disney strategy up in a way that you will *live this enriched* life based on the foundation of break throughs step by step expanding.

Are you ready to unchain the power of your future?

I sense a wave of curiosity building up as you instantly enter the needed internal state easily knowing what to do unconsciously right from the start.

Here we go:

1) Choose a location that represents you at the present – your current here and now.

2) Establish contact with your vision/dream you are about to manifest, ask your unconscious to assist the perfect way it always does and as you look around find a space/location in the future where your dream already has come true, where your vision has manifested excellently.

3) Use your knowledge about submodalities and enhancement and turn that representation of "dream came true" into a sensual extravaganza, full of vibrant energy and sizzling abundance. Double the feelings and double them again. Be creative, use 100s of speakers, choir, a crowd celebrating and cheering you on– whatever comes to mind to turn the experience into ecstasy.

4) Walk towards the space and associate with it, experience the momentum out of your own eyes, let the gorgeous feelings fill you up completely as you absorb all insight and information that might occur out of this future space.

5) Breathing deeply and intensely relaxed, look towards the present (where you located the present) and imagine a path unfolding, a magical indestructible connection between your "dream came true" future and the present.

Notice a special part of your body where this powerful connection anchors itself in your body nourishing your dreamer and realist from inside out. Knowing that this energy will protect your visions and dreams, driving and pushing you towards abundant every-day life.

Notice a path unfolding from future to present. This path consists of a series of actions representing significant steps towards success and manifestation. Make sure that the connection is complete.

6) Go with the flow and follow your intuition and unconscious guidance as you look and walk towards the present collecting and integrating significant steps that logically lead to fulfillment, completion and manifestation of your dream.

7) Take care that you *integrate these gems into your action plan* knowing that these gifts you are giving to yourself now will inevitably *lead to manifestation* of your vision/dream.

8) Arriving at the present location feel how all the new information and new knowledge merges and melts with your personality as you make this your own success assets. Take your time and return fully awakened, fresh and full of power, ready to take action with determination and pride.

•   Enjoy a break, fresh air, some nourishing food as you develop attitude of gratitude that everything unfolds according to a special

master plan for your phenomenal life on your highway to excellence.

Wow, how does that feel to have the resources and unlimited power from the future as your true ally?

This upgrade pattern is definite magic in action. Experiencing your daily life as you apply the new integrated knowledge will add a special jackpot and true wealth to your happily unfolding life. There won't ever be an area of your life where you can't put this to excellent use.

Problem solving, truly enhanced relationships, extremely boosted expertise in whatever business you might be in – there are no limits where and when to apply these wonders of the human mind and mastery.

So many people struggle, crave and long for solutions to their problems and you? Just go into the future in your mind entering a space or location where problems are solved perfectly, utterly creatively and elegantly with solutions that you will apply effectively whenever needed.

Isn't it a fascinating fact after all that you will become an expert in less time than some people need to eat a delicious sandwich?

Well talking about sandwiches – a few days ago I invited Dan and his crew to check how things were going regarding their "journey" of the lifetime.

The actual status of the project surprised me very much.
We made a bunch of seductive sandwiches, some bowls with fresh fruits and other ingredients which you would never have a chance to resist, enjoying life as a magnetically inviting dinner.

Dan and his friends presented the plan to me with enthusiasm.

"Look Dad, I was the dreamer, you know…made the vision and also used your great tips every now and then. You might remember how the "how hammer" was silenced?

Then Tony – our man for the action plan designed the necessary steps to make it all happen, so that we could organize and structure the journey, giving our project shape and manifestation.

See how amazing the 6 weeks will be?

Do you think the story boarding you told us about was effective? If it would be your journey, Dad, what would you say about the plan?"

"First of all guys I'd like to say that you all did an amazing job so far.

The whole project reminds me of the excellent strategy famous Walt Disney used to build his company, solve his problems and most of all created such a bunch of amazing movies.

There was the dreamer being responsible for the vision, the realist having to manage the task of exploration and organizing and the so called critic. The critic only had to focus on the end result and evaluate if this was perfect.

So as I am able to watch you guys from a distance let me see whether there is something to criticize as if I would be your worst nightmare.

This evaluation might enhance your plan even more by letting Dan dream about my ideas and to give Tony more input to boost the plan again. What do you guys think about it?"

Nearly in unison all shouted: "That's gorgeous and exciting, please continue!"

"Well guys let me check – your vision and plan needs to meet certain criteria to be perfect. All three of you want to experience the journey of a lifetime and maybe you have different expectations what that means. I want to walk in everyone's shoes, so to speak, for a while. Tell me guys what is most important for you during the journey?"

"Hmm I want to see many different things and locations!" my son shouted with excitement.

"I am looking forward to enjoying evenings where we have fun together as crew," replied Tony.

"For me it's extremely important that we fulfill the tasks needed to maintain everything nicely like dishes, driving and stuff. Don't want to do that all by myself," was Richard's remark.

I checked the plan and looked at it from a distance to see if the whole project would be working or if something was missing. I played the role of the guy's worst nightmare perfectly, where even Richards Mum would be nothing compared to me in terms of criticism.

Of course the major difference was that my task was to turn any criticism into how questions for the dreamer (Dan) that he could come up with a vision or insight Tony (the realist) could organize and add it to the plan.

It is important to mention that I acknowledged the great work the guys did to come up with this amazing plan and concept intensely and to be honest, due to excellent work performed the weeks ago, I did not find much to criticize.

"Well guys, I am impressed in a way I never thought possible before.

I am completely confident, that this will be the journey of your life so far.

Take one or two days to work with my bits of constructive criticism to let Dan have a dream and vision about it, hand over the results to Tony and come to me then to have a last "critic" check on it."

The room nearly was on fire because of the positive excitement the guys radiated and I guess I do not tell you a secret by revealing that everything got my green light and go signal after I checked again a few days later.

The guys had performed the Disney strategy right from the start having avoided something you also avoided from manual page one (never let the realist or critic interfere or mingle with the dreamer to avoid the death of a vision or dream whereas its destiny is to be manifested in your reality on the sparkling highway to excellence).

I definitely do not cross a line here by telling you that the journey turned out even better than everyone expected. Each day had been a complete joyride. The guys functioned perfectly as a team and everybody's needs have been satisfied phenomenally.

After some days of celebration after his return, Dan told me that he'd never thought that dreaming, preparation and organizing would be so important.

He especially liked my evaluation which provided some very useful input for the fine tuning.

"This especially took care of the success because looking at the whole thing from a distance was so excellent. I could work magnificently with your criticism turned into how questions let me come up with additional solutions.

We had a wonderful start and the great feelings multiplied each day. We could count on each other and I will always remember this brilliantly manifested journey as epic. Many many thanks for your expert help Dad!"

Of course I was very happy to hear these words – the same way I will be happy to read and hear your many success stories as you apply, integrate and use all the knowledge for many dreams and visions already waiting to enrich your life with abundance and wealth in many ways.

Let's sum up the use of the last module of the Disney strategy

Exercise

Utilizing the Critic

Please keep in mind, that the critic never has the task to spoil or destroy your dream. The only and highly important assignment the critic has to perform brilliantly is to take care that everything brings up the best possible result.

As you incorporate the key factors of the strategy, be reminded of the fact that this is not about criticizing the dreamer or the realist – it is about constructively criticizing the plan.

To do this the critic has to have enough distance from the other two to see the whole process evaluating constructively whether something is needed or missing.

Disney is said to have had a room with a huge one sided glass window you might be familiar with from the movies. This location enabled him to look at the dreamer and realist without being to close. That's what I call superb – don't you agree?

• Find a location where you can look at the process from a distance being able to evaluate it constructively.

• Anchor the location applying your mastery in anchoring like you did before so efficiently.

Think of a time where you were able to criticize a plan constructively, a time you are in the flow to come up with missing pieces of a plan, where you just found problems and weakness of a plan.

3) Enhance with submodalities that you feel like the critic expert number one and anchor this state to the location also using a key word and a special gesture.

•   Evaluate the plan/process and write down the found weaknesses or bits that you consider to be missing to make the plan absolutely perfect. Step out of the location into your "Meta" position where you can look at all three location/states – the neutral place and take a break enjoying that you now have mastered it all – congrats to your MHTE degree – Master Highway To Excellence.

5) After the break turn the found missing pieces into "how" questions for the dreamer to come up with new ideas and solutions to make it all truly perfect.

•   Just go for it and manifest your abundance day by day.

Infinite Universe, Boundless Possibilities and Human Evolution Unfolding

How great do you feel right now?

Maybe it's been the journey of your lifetime in terms of learning and personal enhancement?

I knew right from the start that you would perform and participate outrageously and I also knew deep inside myself that I would be right.

My utter appreciation and congrats are with you. I also know that your unconscious will assist you frequently on your way as you enjoy a more and more abundant life, because that is exactly what you deserve and what you are able to unfold out of your limitless potential.

As a feeling of pride, a sense of adventure and curiosity (you remember thumb and index finger!) and many visions may accompany you already preparing to solve the next problem

(maybe you become a professional problem solver making a lot of growing income counseling others?), getting ready to make yet another dream come true or manifest a new vision, I have to tell you something special to round it all up with sparkles and brilliant perspectives.

Have you ever asked yourself: "Hmm what might StClair's mind be like and what is going on inside his brain when he manifests a dream?"

Your wish is my command.

Take a deep breath and follow me to experience a blueprint of my universe as I provide you with the option to acknowledge a building craving to learn more and more by now.

A few months ago I had an exciting conversation with a Facebook contact (also an NLP trainer) and as we felt an amazing energy unleash we decided to team up creating a gorgeous product enabling you to become a master of your own life being able to adopt highly efficient and result producing mindsets of genius and billionaires.

I instantly felt my attitude of gratitude to always meet the right people at the right time and immediately after I have made a clear commitment and decision to create something that is devoted to the purpose of adding value to others I see everything needed fall into place.

I went to my favorite place where all manifestation in my life is blissfully prepared – my inner universe of light and abundance. Inside my mind I have a universe consisting of infinite realms, cities and regions at my convenience – a world constantly in the process of creation, expanding and sizzling energy.

I enjoyed a special state of deep relaxation and entered my inner time machine letting it beam me to a day where this product was finished and completed in a much more excellent way that I would have been able to imagine at the time of traveling.

I met my future self who had created the product and merged with it collecting all needed information that would lead me to a state where only I would have the chance to move towards the goal manifesting this product with my best skills and abilities as your brilliant coach and trainer.

As I looked back towards my present I saw the most significant ideas and steps driving me forward, inspiring me and letting me put all these onto paper and on audios to provide subscribers with multiple sensory learning experience where I took care excellently for their success.

You see – your success already was sealed and highly important for me before I even wrote the first letter.

Next was to enter the ultimate city of creativity to meet some genius minds from my mentor team. I have thousands of mentors I can meet at my convenience and to ensure the product to be amazing I met Walt Disney and two other geniuses that had extremely effective impact on our world in terms of creativity.

I told them about the product and let them each unfold a vision about it, asked them to provide me with the essence of their work and incorporated this essence in a way that I could include everything in the product.

This felt magnificent beyond words and not only because it happened in minutes but it gifted me a rush of energy that was simply awesome.

Shortly after this experience I entered my castle of planning.

I have the perfect place to organize and structure my plans and visions to chop them into small steps I easily can transform into action and manifestation in my reality.

Carrying the plan with me I met my ultimate expert of constructive criticism asking to find some potential problems, weaknesses or if there would be something missing.

This review let me come up with the many resources and additional ideas how to enhance this course even more.

Live training, radio show and webinars should ensure that you would profit from my wizard like experience and skills directly in contact with your master coach in live situations to feel the comfort that each of your questions and concerns could be addressed and flexibly be taken care of.

This led me to the idea of my 24/7 communication server where subscribers can talk with other subscribers and members to support each other or just have fun sharing experiences along the way.

For many it is a wonderful resource to be in the middle of companions for only 29.95$ a month additional forum fee. (For those who did not sign up for the 8 week Mindset Masters Volume One course interacting directly 101 with us daily – subscribers enjoy free access during the course)

This paragraph is only valid for subscribers of my online course!!

The fact that I also open up the option for phone hypnosis, direct 1 on 1 training with a limited amount and the possibility for you to hire me as short or longer term project coach serves the ultimate bouquet for you where you only have to choose what to enjoy first.

Filled up with a feeling of completion, satisfaction and gratitude I allow myself to let joy overflow in me as I go through the circle dreamer – realist – critic a few times using the feelings of joy and gratitude as a foundation.

This ensures lateral thinking and unconscious gestation.
Then I just go for it and now here I am there for you as you celebrate your success maybe forever and a day?

All the best and to your abundance and success,

David John W. StClair

For 101 sessions or in case of any question contact me here:

support@mindsetmasters.net

Bonus Section

David John StClair

Interviewed by

Allison Williams Hill

To get to know me even better, to dive more into my personality as well as to enjoy the different approaches I apply to unfold my effectiveness for each company and client here is the newest interview I have been featured in.

This has been an amazing talk with Allison Williams Hill – enjoy!

Interview with Allison Williams Hill (http://www.in-vesica.com)

AWH: Thank you, David John, for agreeing to be interviewed. Your personal description is provocative to the extent that I think people are ready to learn more about it. You have been providing personal performance and strategies services since 1994 to athletes, companies and individuals. What drove you to doing this work?

David John: Thank you very much Allison for giving me the chance to enjoy this interview with you. Interesting question – what drove me?

In 1986 I opened my private practice as an acupuncturist, natural healer using herbs, homeopathy, the energies of flower essences like the Bach Flower remedies and many more.

Maybe I am allowed to go a little more back. 1980 I became a male nurse and the first impression during the education was a colleague who cleaned a urine bottle as if he would have to save the world by the way HOW he would do things.

This was like a celebration for him. I learned very much from this man.

After some years of private practice from 1986 – 1990 I went to university to study "conventional medicine". During semester holidays I studied NLP (Neuro Linguistic Programming) and Ericksonian Hypnosis very intensely.

The really big shift was inspired after I became a NLP trainer. I only wanted to learn from the best, so I decided to experience the "Lion King of change" himself Dr. Richard Bandler, the Co-Creator of NLP.

After the first 3 weeks with Richard (Hypnosis, D.H.E. [his invention Design Human Engineering] and trainers training) I faced the alternative going back to medicine study or become a Bandler associate to train and work with CEOs, companies and each individual I met who wanted to enhance life towards desired goals or living dreams.

So the external input was how Richard enhanced my life with his passion and commitment to let everybody lead a better life. I'm very thankful for the honor to have been chosen to assist him during his seminars in Germany for a few years.

AWH: Over the last 15 years, have you noticed a change in the clientele or in people you intuit need service and support with respect to world change?

David StClair: Definitely YES Allison. Since the real estate and Wall Street shifts happened there is much more insecurity. Many people seem to crave for direction having lost faith in their own genius and enormous power. No matter how the circumstances are, you are always able to act and react with creativity, flexibility and optimism. To make my point a bit clearer: Optimism and focused will create the energies for personal change.

There is a huge difference between a wish ("Oh how I wish that things might change!") or "I have the utter and determined will for change!"

Sometimes you have to force luck and destiny to act according your will by living the attitude that you never ever will accept another outcome.

Poverty consciousness, fear of failure, self - doubt – all these limiting and distracting energies are no option.

So one main focus is based on a "Phoenix approach". Assisting people to rise out of the ashes of a limiting self-image, paralyzing beliefs, melting adopted stuff which is of no use anymore.

We are all manifested consciousness of LOVE or call it of The ALL there is or GOD. Consider yourself as a temple for the only energy that conquers everything.

Ages ago in front of the hidden caves of initiation there was written "Know thyself and you know the world!" This sums it up pretty well.

An attitude of gratitude and a growing awareness of your own eternity is a phenomenal support. How do you feel thinking that each day is a white page in your book of life you can inscribe and imprint with your love, zest for life, kindness and devotion to joy and creation.

AWH: You shared "... a few driving words (you) live by: „The greatest love adventure is life itself."" How do you live your life to experience each moment, each day as an adventure?

David John: Thank you very much Allison for bringing this question up. First of all I will consider myself to be an eternal beginner and student of life. Gandhi was once asked how he looked at himself, how he did living his teachings. As far as I remember he answered (no precise quote here) "Oh he definitely wasn't the best – just an eternal beginner."

I am grateful to live surrounded by nature, many trees, 5-7 cats (some stepping by every now and then to grab some cuddles before they head off to mouse hunt again) and most importantly with my family and gorgeous unique friends.

My every day life is based on an advice from a person I spiritually owe everything I am. "Concentrate on the obvious and self evident." Taken into account that your actions are morally and ethically responsible Allison, it really does not matter what you do. What matters is HOW you do it.

I love keeping things easily and effective. I firmly believe that it's of no advantage to be born in certain families or countries regarding your chances to evolve on your earth's path here. No doubt that life circumstances and some countries might make it harder but back to the HOW.

Perform every action with a love as if the destiny of the universe depends on how you do it. It's a matter of "tuning in".

In the beginning it was quite a challenge to bind shoes with love, to take out trash as if the universe depends on my love doing it. And there would be many examples.

How would you brush your teeth differently if the universe's existence depended on it?

That's exactly one of the most excellent power sources we humans possess. Who of your very appreciated readers might be familiar with the karma concept (Every cause has an effect and every action has an energy coming back to you) can imagine how much energy, chances and power is in your hands every single day.

Feed your pets with love, smile at your neighbor with love, help your kids with homework as if the universe depends on your attitude – this is a powerful wave where the law of attraction hype is a mouse compared to a dinosaur.

Concentrating on your every single action gives you the gift of instant pleasure feedback loop as each action nurtures your soul immediately.

Please understand me right. I am far from living in a state of eternally experienced bliss as every day life and its duties sometimes distract or let me become less sensible for my path,

but experiencing myself once again in the described state of "complete awareness" leads me back deep inside where I never left my eternal home and origin.

AWH: Do you impart that approach to your clients?

David John: Absolutely Allison, there is no other option than to walk the talk. It is so fundamentally important to remind my clients that they are in control, have the momentum always at their side being able to change life for the better any minute.

No matter how you look at your life – the best place and time to begin to live your dreams is here and now.

Whether it's a company looking for new approaches to sell, new creativity strategies, effective ways to streamline and improve employee motivation – whether a couple wants to multiply intimacy and love or a single person feels the desire to live life from an eternal perspective I am respectfully up to a break- through for everyone.

You know awakening, enlightenment can be a spontaneous process as someone recognizes that he is no victim anymore but a unique gem that is so important. One drop more can be the start to let a flower grow in a desert.

Living life out of these attitudes and beliefs exactly will ignite the ground breaking energies that open the gates for abundance.

When it comes to life design I effectively assist clients/companies in living the best possible "YOU" that can be imagined. Then we take this as a foundation for more and more to come. Personal excellence and mastery is a process that lasts as long as your life and I am happy to assist in every imaginable way.

Like Einstein said "Gods thoughts are simple" it's my attitude to install and pack things not only in design that works but also can be understood and lived by a professor the same way as if a person who has never seen anyone before without education would have to understand it.

AWH: I appreciate how you described your life as "…a bouquet of different colors. Does this describe the Rainbow Concept?

David John: Hmm I appreciate these challenging questions and I hope I answer them to the benefit of every reader.
The rainbow concept indeed is the actual foundation and essence of what I teach.

The rainbow concept is based on my book "Living The Rainbow" a series of seven books where I am working on volume two and three at the same time as volume two got lost in a hard disk crash and I did not save it before – so I got the chance to rewrite it discovering some great new aspects feeling my characters in a completely new way.

EHFTB – FTWMIH (Everything happens for the best – for those who make it happen).

It's not life and experiences that create pain – it's the perception how we look at life and how we judge things. Beginning 2011 The Rainbow Concept" will be launched as a unique coaching program that can't be compared to anything on the market so far. If you wish I will be happy to provide a chapter for your readers as a preview

AWH: You state that you activate the inner hero. How do you help clients find and even embrace their inner hero?
David John: I am completely aligned with Sheldrake's morphogenetic fields. We definitely are all connected.

I also believe that there is something like a global mind or a universal human consciousness affecting us. Compare it to a radio station where you have the ability to tune in to every station as the radio is influenced by every input but it depends on your inner focus and direction which "wave family" you belong to.

Your thoughts are like an ox you tie in front of a plow. Loose focus and goal out of sight and you don't need to wonder why you find yourself at another destination than the desired one. One chapter of volume 2 compares it with an infinite field of golden micro stars – the particles defining infinite possible futures.

The more energy and thoughts you focus on certain things the more density evolves until the process of manifestation happens. Here we touch a very essential point.

I see a huge danger hiding behind the law of attraction hype. In NLP we say the map is not the territory which means there is no objective perception but only individual perception through our filters (through values, beliefs and aspects like generalization, deletion [important facts are blended or left out] for example.

It might sound so attractive to say "you can achieve everything you want", but can you imagine the consequences for a fifty year old intending to win the gold medal next Olympics 100 meter sprint?

This whole "you can achieve everything thing" is similar to the snake telling Adam and Eve "sicut deus eritis" (you'll be like God). This "movement" puts heavy pressure on people who don't have race car or super villa after some months of intense "attraction" and secondly it seduces to focus on material things only. Too many people crave for being a millionaire falling into the "fear and greed" cycle and ending up disappointed.

In my now over 30 years of experience with these topics it's the other way round.

The universe or the ultimate love behind it loves us unconditionally in a way that we all deserve and shall have abundance – definitely.

The question is to ask the right questions. Instead of striving through life asking "sh…t what is my life's purpose or the general purpose of life" ask what can I do to BE a purpose. Many people don't know how intensely others might wait for their smile, consolation or assistance.
Concentrating on the self - evident always hands over the golden key into the individuals hands.

First heal yourself, family, friends. Every action driven by love will have huge impact beyond imagination and it's in front of your eyes each day.

Everybody can change the world for the better by improving bit by bit day by day.
But back to the inner hero Allison. I believe and feel that our origin is rooted in realms where we had power beyond belief becoming afraid of it.

Finding the inner hero means stop searching outside when everything you desire and much much more resides deep very deep inside you.

It might sound complicated to say that it is easier to lead a wild elephant on a rope through a store full of china than to enter these inner regions of the soul but what do I talk about ?

Even LoA (Law of Attraction) is often based on brain based concepts. The inner hero – someone asked once: "What is love?" and the answer my guide gave was "you will know the moment you have transformed into love – the moment you became love. So the inner hero is something only to be found inside.

Imagine a "hortus conclusus" which is Latin and means closed garden. How do you enter something that you can't enter from the outside?

You have to enter it from WITHIN (where the keys reside) I am trying to find words for experiences which are unique for each soul on earth and abundance, wealth, happiness in fact is all about love….how to access the states that transform you automatically from inside out.

The true secrets and mankind's most profound and deepest knowledge can't be revealed through brain based exploration. It can be experienced, individually felt and lived.

Imagine a dome made of each soul currently living. We mentioned that we are all connected (wave family) based on your stage of development etc..

How would that dome look if everybody wanted to be a corner stone? An Orchestra made to rejoice creation where everybody wanted to be a guitar?

Probably one of the greatest mysteries and revelations might be hidden in the fact that happiness, abundance and life's purpose can be lived and "earned" just where you are out of each moment (through attitude and the determination to live life as an art) as we are all artists of our life.

Consider the place where you are right now as the place to be, as the place to love and to evolve being the stone in this dome where you are meant to be.

AWH: Given the various experiences people come to you with, how do you penetrate the layers to reach that soul? (You may wish to include the many different techniques, combinations you employ because each person is unique).

David John: The HOW? I adjust that personally during the first contact with a client and the many sessions I regularly experience with many clients show that I only have to enter a state of deep listening, open up my heart for the other and create a space that belongs only to me and the other one(s).

Then all what's needed reveals itself automatically.

Whether I use hypnosis, techniques from Kahuna, Shamanism, N.L.P. D.H.E. or N.H.R (Neuro Hypnotic Repatterning -----> Richard Bandlers' newest invention and approach to achieve rapid long lasting change) or many other tools too many to mention is secondary in nature.

My job is to be an assistant along the way with competence and love as the guidance watching over us all assists to let the miracle happen and life is transformed groundbreaking and healing on an ongoing basis.

A few words describe significantly a main approach: Layering responses, propulsion systems and individual holistic system.

Layering responses means to use many different tools, techniques and approaches all aiming at the formerly agreed outcome/goal. Brain – unconscious – body-mind - soul connection are some golden keys.

As I see each person as a unique individual (companies, families and couples as teams) each evolving path also will be a unique one.
Propulsion system describes a set up where a client automatically moves towards desired goals with magnetically attracting lust and pleasure. Here the question: How much pleasure can a person stand becomes important.

AWH: I read your articles at Ezine. I liked the fact you included one about an individual's transformation and another about a business. You wrote: "Making money is like any other skill set. You don't need to stop being yourself in order to learn it - you just need to open your mind to thinking about your life in brand new ways." That's a great statement- concise and to the point. (Please comment.)

David John: As simple this may sound Allison, yes that's the way I see and sense it. It is never about stop being yourself. It is about expand the map of your world how you perceive it.

Try something new until you find what works and add this to your repertoire and continue this way.

Based on the topics I talked about in earlier questions a sense of adventure, boundless curiosity and the "wings of love" will nourish along the way. There are infinite ways to think about your life. Do it in a way that will lead you to results and towards your visions and dreams.

AWH: I also saw you have a CD "Dreams Come True". I heard the sample. It was elevating and had a nice rhythm. Something I could listen to while driving. Do you use this with clients? Did you find it would be a positive offering to the public at large?

David John: "Dreams Come True" definitely is my best English spoken work so far (I also made 7 CDs in German before).Based on a sports metaphor the CD is a very good example of my hypnotic work, how I use language, tonality, voice tempo etc. in change work.

Only looking at these facts the CD has a lot of potential to enrich everybody and the topic "Let your dreams come true!" isn't unattractive either and looking at the sales and feedback I received so far by now it is worth to be checked out by everyone interested in doing themselves a favor to enjoy very relaxing moments and amazing energies to live your dreams towards your desired directions.

That's why the CD is sold world - wide and available at CD Baby right here:

http://www.cdbaby.com/AlbumDetails.aspx?AlbumID=jwstclair

AWH: IS there anything you would like to add?

David John: Thank you very much for this great interview with very profound and challenging questions. Answering them has been a great adventure to me.

First of all I would love to thank my friends and family for all their support letting me be the way I am living my life's purpose here on earth.

Secondly a call to everyone having the honor to live with animals like cats, dogs or horses. (or others of course).

Consider your companions to be a teacher and treat them with respect and love. I am very grateful for what I am learning daily from my cats. A special thank you goes out to friends and colleagues who support and inspire me like Victoria Vives, James Goi jr., Stephen Brooks, Dr. Carlos Gonzalez, my soul sister Julie P (wouldn´t know where I would be without your energies and support!) and every expert friend listed at my new site:

http://www.mastermind.olympus.com

(changed into the newest site
http://www.mindsetmasters.net)

Everybody is invited to enter their email for inspiring newsletters and free gifts as well as I love to read comments on blog articles.

Precise info also soon to be found at my site.

Of course a very big thanks to YOU Allison for the wonderful opportunity and invitation to enjoy this interview. All the best to you and your readers with my best wishes!

AWH: How can someone reach you?

David John: The best way is to contact me at:

support@mindsetmasters.net

As I offer also skype coaching, email and phone sessions this email will be the best for a first contact to proceed then in mutual agreement about next steps. Precise info about coaching sessions also can be found at my site.

How to change Beliefs in an instant

Beliefs are subjective ideas about what is true or not true for our perception of the world. We develop beliefs through exposure to experience modified by our perceptual filters of generalization, deletion and distortion.

Utilizing my live webinars or trainings included in the premium subscription you will enjoy extreme assistance to change beliefs the way you want to.

An impressive example how to change belief easily is given in my recently published successful article below – enjoy!

A good friend of mine I appreciate very much told me that she felt like held back by some limiting beliefs she truly did not want in her life anymore. She compared her experience with a tree - the trunks being the beliefs. Some trunks may be outdated or not useful but still influencing the whole tree.

Looking at the tree with anticipation this reminded me of the fact how easily people can go into a trance without even having noticed at exactly what point the best and deep rooted feeling of relaxation had begun to spread throughout the whole body.

As I was looking at the tree I felt comfortable to forget that something wonderful already had taken care of my nurturing breathing. this wonderfully supporting in and out providing the most useful oxygen for a magical day to come.

I sometimes enjoy stepping back a few steps to gain new perspectives as I feel safe that my unconscious takes care of all my learning as I remember some other meanings of the tree.

Just like the tree I am a spiritual being rooted deeply in my basic utter trust in life that my core always will have enough water to be nurtured - and I don't care whether it's through inspiring words coming from friends, through a smile coming from a child having fun at the playground nearby or from the idea that it's playfulness infected me with curiosity this morning.

What if I just could remember some magical spells from the past I forgot a while ago that would be the most useful right now. What was it I already knew I didn't know yet 10 minutes ago what had helped me to try the most useful beliefs I had not tried before? The child had forgotten time as if diving deep into playfulness had ignited a sort of healing time distortion to think as if magical moments of easily change now into desired directions would last forever.
The child eyes looked at me saying: "I knew you would remember that your inside influences the outside and as if letting your boundless love shine would have made the sun come up to warm you smoothly.

This magical truth in the eyes of a child. How could I forget that the sun comes up every day reminding me of my grandpa's belief that there will always be a guiding light in life!

Some months ago my unconscious applied for a new job and inspired me to free some space inside for a positive change inside that would carry me with love and faith for the rest of my long, happy and abundant life. It said: "Hey I have energy left for something special to let the tree be filled with light and love so what do you want me to do to let you feel the old things you don't need anymore leave with respect as I replace it with new beliefs attracting you into your desired future you closer to live your visions and dreams?"

Well how would the child have responded? I looked at it playing as it suddenly had found a diamond hidden in the sand. The child's face turned into pure satisfaction and pleasure and I saw excellent feelings spread and double every 10 minutes as the child explored the question: How much pleasure can you stand?

Did I hear the question right or was there something more left to do? No matter from what side the inspiration bubbles up from my unconscious I suddenly could answer the question smoothly: "So what about installing a master belief that I quit "buying" limitations that don't do any good to me as I decided to only accept suggestions letting me open up for the wise master plan unfolding inside of me as the diamond from the sand threw a sparkle of bliss inside the change towards me.

"I can do that", my unconscious responded. "But is that all you can come up with? Come on I challenge you as the tree already has begun to let limiting beliefs respectfully dissolve in the past as you respectfully keep the learning supporting you utterly awesome here."

"You want it, you got it ", I smiled and then I asked my unconscious the following: "what about getting rid of limiting fears keeping me back from the success I so richly now deserve?"

My unconscious smiled again: "well useful paradox cushions can heal inside as I replace limiting fears with a fear of fearing the fear of keeping back in a way that only the pleasure of your supporting healthy self image allowing that limitations vanish easily in a way that the former fear had turned into the Sherlock Holmes energy.

Where once was limiting fear there now is the sense of adventure to find new ways of living abundance, exploring new ways to find diamonds inside as the tree carries the most delicious fruits ready to be harvested at your convenience.

Holmes once was a learning beginner in the field of old beliefs can be replaced easily with strong positive new ones as my unconscious scored the win completely: Hey need sumptin' more now?

I give you a bonus: I gift you the believe that limiting beliefs will be out of reach for you forever and if you love candy here is the easily believe change chewing gum. As you taste the magic I will try some fun for you within the next days. I will try an "unconscious positive believe changer".

Whenever some rotten relict of old limiting stuff might be found in your depths I instantly will replace them with really kicking positive beliefs according to your inner master plan - whatcha think?"
I looked at the tree and noticed that there was a healing connection between the tree and the whole forest - light emerging from each tree through all others and vice versa. Everything was connected and love shining and radiating from me became a benefit for each tree as I was nurtured by their love.

My tree instantly looked so unique, rich, abundant and healed that I gave my unconscious thumbs up: "Go for it buddy as I have to enjoy each step of my journey to enjoy myself as a wonderful unique being learning that I deserve the best!"

As I had looked at the tree now completely healed and prepared to shelter me from every possible storm as long as eternity would last I noticed the child right in front of me hugging me.
"See my friend that was not hard at all to enjoy that invitation to heal the tree, wasn't it?"

"Hehe", I replied "I just wanted to read xxxx's entry at Facebook".

"Wasn't that cool", the child smiled at me chewing a gum. You don't need to know consciously that blissful change always is just around the corner!"

Links and Contact

http://www.mindsetmasters.net (Main product site)

Facebook Profile:

http://www.facebook.com/profile.php?id=100000802789064

Facebook Fanpage for the products produced with my close friend and http://www.sqr.fm radio host colleague Tammra Broughton --------> Broughton/StClair Productions: Please push the like button and IN Joy

http://www.facebook.com/pages/BroughtonStClair-Productions/251819878174190

email: support@mindsetmasters.net

Special Recommendation:

Join http://www.sqr.fm (Spirit Quest and life altering talk radio with many gifted and amazing hosts. You also can skype in and participate in the many radio shows daily or just listen world wide for free over the internet)

Products:

Mindset Masters - Walt Disney

CD one from the Mindset Masters Walt Disney mindset. Awaken the dreamer and turn your visions into manifested actions and outrageous success.

Also look out for CD 2 (the realist realm)

A must have for everybody interested in personal excellence, self improvement, NLP, hypnosis and an abundant life to attract joy, success and whatever you crave for. Highly recommended to massively boost the success of this program.

Order here:

http://www.createspace.com/1907316

Mindset Masters Walt Disney 2

Welcome to the second bonus CD from the mindset masters series featuring Walt Disney mindset for excellent creative problem solving and utter creativity. CD one awakened the dreamer.
This CD here will teleport you into the realist realm to get your visions and dreams into manageable pieces speeding up manifestation instantly. Another piece of art from NLP trainer and mindset master David John W. StClair

https://www.createspace.com/1907317

Vibrant Health

Broughton/StClair

Radio Talk Show Hosts, NLP Experts and Coaches Tammra Broughton and David John W. StClair join forces to add huge value and inspiration to your life. 10 specially designed and mixed affirmations assist you instantly to re-program your health, activate your inner healing code and improve your overall fitness. Smooth daytime listening during breakfast, work out or recreational minutes uplift and direct towards a wonderful life.

CreateSpace eStore: https://www.createspace.com/1984807

Wealth and Money Magnet Daytime meditation

Broughton/StClair

Become a money magnet and turn yourself into a superb attractor factor for wealth. Your Radio Talk Show Hosts and Internet Personalities Tammra Broughton and David John StClair created a highly efficient meditation that lets you manifest wealth and attract money like a huge magnet.

CreateSpace eStore: https://www.createspace.com/1984884

Wealth and Money Magnet Deep Relaxation Edition

Broughton/StClair

Become a money magnet and turn yourself into a superb attractor factor for wealth. Your Radio Talk Show Hosts and Internet Personalities Tammra Broughton and David John StClair created a highly efficient meditation that lets you manifest wealth and attract money like a huge magnet. Special deep relaxation edition with extra mixed brainwaves - theta for pleasant listening before sleep or to relax deeply as manifestation becomes joyful reality.

CreateSpace eStore: https://www.createspace.com/1984980

Mindset Masters - Abundance Affirmations

David John W.StClair

Mindset Masters bring you Affirmations of Abundance. Each track is around 4 minutes long and can be used to start with positivity, motivation, determination and pleasure into an outrageous day towards increasing abundance.

CreateSpace eStore: https://www.createspace.com/1961795

Core Transformation Volume One

David John W, StClair

Welcome to David John W. StClair`s Core transformation series. "Letters to everyone" Benefit from NLP Trainer Master skills and specific nested loop metaphorical hypnosis. Volume 1-3 feature the core transformation of a famous author and sales trainer who suddenly had to face the diagnosis leukemia. Witness the transformation from programmed stressful fight or flight response to oneness applying state of the art NLP and hypnosis techniques, quantum healing, prayers and much more. Besides that its all about your personal journey to oneness and the mindset of self healing. Listen with anticipation as you discover that each line has found you by now with a specific purpose - realizing that today is the day where your alignment with your source and what you internally already have become has begun now!Healing inside out.

CreateSpace eStore: https://www.createspace.com/1991005

Core Transformation Vol. one - nighttime

David John W. StClair

Deep Relaxation edition

CreateSpace eStore: https://www.createspace.com/1991391

Core Transformation Volume two

David John W. StClair

Welcome to David John W. StClairs Core transformation series. "Letters to everyone" Benefit from NLP Trainer Master skills and specific nested loop metaphorical hypnosis. Volume 1-3 feature the core transformation of a famous author and sales trainer who suddenly had to face the diagnosis leukemia. Witness the transformation from programmed stressful fight or flight response to oneness applying state of the art NLP and hypnosis techniques, quantum healing, prayers and much more. Besides that it's all about your personal journey to oneness and the mindset of self healing. Listen with anticipation as you discover that each line has found you by now with a specific purpose - realizing that today is the day where your alignment with your source and what you internally already have become has begun now!

This is Volume two - **Journey to a calm and gentle YOU**. The author who faced the diagnosis leukemia decided he did not need to have control over everything and he needed to be more calm and gentle with himself - listen, relax and experience the transformation happening with bliss

CreateSpace eStore: https://www.createspace.com/1991144

Core Transformation Vol. two - nighttime

David John W. StClair

Deep Relaxation Edition

CreateSpace eStore: https://www.createspace.com/1991392

Core Transformation Volume Three

David John W. StClair

From dis - ease to oneness

CreateSpace eStore: https://www.createspace.com/1991168

Core Transformation Vol. Three

From Dis-ease to Oneness nighttime

David John W. StClair

Deep Relaxation Edition

CreateSpace eStore: https://www.createspace.com/1991393

There will be frequently added more new products, so please check the Fan page often. The radio shows at http://www.sqr.fm most likely will keep you informed too.

ABOUT THE AUTHOR

David John met his spiritual teacher and guide at an age of 16 opening a path for him to embody his divine light through his thoughts, words and actions.

He once said: "I will always consider myself as an eternal beginner living my life's purpose by being a vessel for this divine energies.

1994 certified as NLP Trainer and Trainer master by Dr. Richard Bandler, certification and intense training in Ericksonian Hypnosis, Hypnotherapy, Persuasion Engineering and DHE, Healing with metaphors and inspirational stories.

Wide experience in coaching (one on one, groups and business leadership management). Own therapy and seminar center training psychologists and other people of many different professions in NLP, hypnosis, communication, creative problem solving, life design and goal achievement.

Producer of CD's "Dreams come true, Abundance Affirmations, Affirmations for vibrant health, Walt Disney mindset bonus trances like Dream Machine and The Realist Realm, book author of "Living the Rainbow Volume one" a new approach to covert and unconscious learning and easy change using different story levels and healing metaphors.

Feel free to schedule a meeting at my cita business page seeing my business hours to set up an appointment for a free informational talk

http://www.vcita.com/experts/195